IPSWICH TRAMWAYS

Colin Barker

Series editor Robert J Harley

MP Middleton Press

Front Cover. Typical of the Ipswich electric rolling stock is this view of Car 12 positioned in Burrell Road for the benefit of the photographer just beyond the railway station on the left. The car terminated at the station on the shuttle from Cornhill in the town centre as indicated by the destination board above the between decks advertisement; cars had to run to this point to reverse at certain times before the 1914/18 War. The three storey houses to the rear are now mainly flats. (Author's postcard)

Rear Cover: Car 33 is in an advanced state of restoration by a small dedicated team at the Ipswich Transport Museum located in the old trolleybus depot in Cobham Road. The ingenuity of the team in reproducing the various detailed items is commendable and is to a quality standard achieved by professional restorers. Details of the museum's activities and opening days can be seen at www. ipswichtransportmuseum.co.uk (Ipswich Transport Museum)

Cover colours: These reflect the tram liveries.

Published June 2009

ISBN 978 1 906008 55 0

© Middleton Press, 2009

Design Deborah Esher

Published by
        Middleton Press
        Easebourne Lane
        Midhurst
        West Sussex
        GU29 9AZ
Tel: 01730 813169
Fax: 01730 812601
Email: info@middletonpress.co.uk
www.middletonpress.co.uk

Printed in the United Kingdom by Henry Ling Limited, at the Dorset Press, Dorchester, DT1 1HD

CONTENTS

INTRODUCTION AND ACKNOWLEDGEMENTS

Following the publication of my book on Ipswich trolleybuses it seemed appropriate to prepare a similar publication on the tramway system that the trolleybuses replaced.

The preparation of this book has been a slow process as Ipswich was one of the earliest United Kingdom municipalities to change from trams to trolleybuses between 1923 and 1926. Therefore photographs of the tramway system taken by enthusiasts are virtually non-existent, and in the main it has been necessary to use official views and commercial postcards. Some of the latter have appeared in 'Ipswich Past' publications over the years but have been consolidated into this single volume to give a more comprehensive picture of the Ipswich horse and electric tram era.

Whilst the advent of the horse tramway system provided a basic public transport operation the introduction of electric trams beyond the original termini, plus the introduction of new routes, gave the general public a cheap, speedy and reliable means of moving around the area, which contributed to the development and expansion of this county town. Before the advent of electric trams the only means of transport was to cycle, be drawn by a horse or have the doubtful benefit of one of the early motorcars.

This publication is not intended to be a definitive history but more a camera shot of public transport and day-to-day life in Ipswich between 1880 and 1926. The views are arranged working outwards from the Cornhill in the centre of the town, which was the focal point of the system, and follow each route in a clockwise direction.

Thanks go to the Ipswich Transport Museum for access to their archive material and to R C Anderson for contributing the route map. Bob Markham, Brian Dyes and Mike Abbott made constructive suggestions on reading through the first draft and thanks go to my wife, Maureen, for her support and her word processing skills to knock my one finger keyboard efforts into shape.

GEOGRAPHICAL SETTING

From the earliest days Ipswich has always been linked to the River Orwell with its access to the East coast, North Sea and near continent. In Saxon times a settlement was established in the area where the River Orwell was fordable.

Ipswich developed as a trading port but stagnated in the eighteenth century. All this changed in the nineteenth century when the river channel was dredged, realigned and the docks developed thus changing this provincial market town, with its decaying port, into an industrial town with busy shipping activity.

The industrial development tended to be in the dock/river area and included manufacturing companies of worldwide fame including Ransomes Sims & Jefferies plus Ransomes & Rapier. Other substantial industries included agricultural fertilizers, milling and malting.

The advent of the railway from London to Colchester in 1846, plus the lines to Bury St Edmunds and Norwich in 1846 and 1849, greatly improved transport facilities in the area, although the original and current station are some way from the town centre.

This rapid development lead to substantial increase in population as people from the country areas moved to the town in search of employment. Thus, by the late nineteenth century, the need for some form of public transport was becoming apparent if the town was to continue to develop.

The terrain around Ipswich is by no means flat and the steepest gradients for horse trams were Mill Street, (later renamed as an extension of Portman Road) and St Johns Road. With the introduction of electric trams Spring Road, Bishops Hill and Bramford Road were added to the list.

HISTORICAL BACKGROUND

The movement of people from the surrounding country areas into Ipswich lead to housing development well beyond the central areas of the town. In the late 1870's this lead to proposals for public transport and in 1879 the Board of Trade gave permission for a horse tramway from Cornhill to the Great Eastern Railway (GER) station.

Construction took place in the Spring/Summer of 1880 to a 3'6" (1067mm) gauge with paving between the track and 18" (457mm) each side. The contractor was declared bankrupt at the end of construction and his rights auctioned and acquired by Simon Armstrong Graham of Manchester.

The service opened on the 13th October 1880 with two single deck cars built by Starbuck of Birkenhead. They were painted brown and cream and seated 18 passengers. The first depot was not built until 1881 and it assumed that cars were parked at the end of the line in the early days. The depot was at the junction of Cardinal Street and New Cardinal Street. A replacement depot was built on the opposite side of New Cardinal Street and eventually closed in June 1903. As late as the early 1990's a haulage contractor used the site with tram track still in evidence.

A second route was opened in March 1881 leaving Princes Street and travelling along Portman Road and Mill Street to Barrack Corner, and thence along Norwich Road as far as Brooks Hall Road. A third car was purchased, this time an open top double decker.

An Act of Parliament incorporated the business as the Ipswich Tramway Company in 1881 with powers to operate additional routes; the Graham rights were acquired at this time. Route extensions followed from Cornhill to Barrack Corner in 1882 and from Majors Corner to Derby Road station in 1883. This left the routes to the east and west of the town centre unconnected and a temporary depot was used adjacent to the Railway Hotel close to Derby Road station. In 1884 the connection was made with track being laid between Cornhill and Majors Corner and this eastern facility closed; this was the final extension of horse tramway that left the system with a total of 4.4 miles (7.1km) of track. By this time a further four single deck and one double deck car had been purchased with the fleet serviced by eighteen horses.

The system operated satisfactorily into the 1890's until a problem arose with the paving between the rails. The section between Cornhill and Barrack Corner used wooden blocks rather than the stone setts used beyond the town centre and they had deteriorated to such an extent Ipswich Corporation requested that they be repaired. The company did not comply and the Corporation carried out the work themselves and sent the bill to the operator. The subsequent dispute between the two parties resulted in services being withdrawn for two weeks.

An additional double deck car was purchased in 1896 bringing the total fleet to nine, and by the end of the decade three single deckers had been converted to double deck format.

In 1898 competition arrived in the form of the Ipswich Omnibus Service that operated a fleet of eighteen red horse drawn buses from a depot in Kemball Street. They operated along the tram routes and into new areas of the town with competitive fares that forced the tramway company to reduce theirs.

Ipswich Corporation obtained powers to establish an electricity undertaking in 1897 and expressed an interest in purchasing the company. The Ipswich Corporation Tramway Act of 1900 gave the municipality powers to operate their own system and served a compulsory purchase order on the company in 1901 under the 1870 Tramway Act provisions. The purchase price was fixed by arbitration at £17,552.

The Corporation took over on 1st November 1901 and continued to operate the horse tramway system. The latter ceased in June 1903 to allow for the speedy installation of cables, track and overhead ready for the electric trams. A site in Constantine Road was purchased, namely Seven Acre Field, for the erection of offices, power station, depot and refuse destructor with construction commencing in 1902. The area was marshy and problems arose with the foundations for the power station chimney stack that resulted in a substantial concrete base to distribute the weight.

Dick Kerr & Company installed the track with wooden blocks or stone setts between and each side of the rails. A 3' 6" (1067mm) gauge was used with a total of 10.8 route miles (17.4km) of which 4.2 miles (6.75km) were double, mainly in the town centre, and the balance single track with passing loops. The British Electrical Company installed the overhead wiring which was mainly suspended by bracket arms. To open the system twenty-six open top double deck cars were purchased from Brush of Loughborough in 1903; a further ten cars arrived the following year. They seated 50 (26 upstairs and 24 inside) and were painted green and cream.

The first trial run to the then village of Whitton was on 10th November 1903, and was an extension of the Norwich Road horse tram route. The first full route conversion from Whitton to Bourne Bridge (Wherstead Road) was inspected by the Board of Trade on 20th November 1903 and passed for public service. The official opening took place the next day when the Lady Mayoress opened the depot doors with a symbolic key, which was followed by a luncheon within the building and a trip along the route.

Public use began on 23rd November along the inspected route, which had a branch along Bath Street to provide access to the River Orwell and the berths for the river steamers that operated to Felixstowe, Harwich and beyond. The branch also served the factory of Ransomes and Rapier.

Further extensions were along Spring Road terminating at the Lattice Barn public house and along Bramford Road as far as the railway over bridge, plus the replacement of the Derby Road Station horse tram route. These opened on 21st December 1903.

These developments, and the extensions opened in 1904, saw the end of the Ipswich Omnibus Service horse buses. In March 1904 the connection was made between the Bell Inn corner on Vernon Street and Princes Street via Stoke Bridge, St Peters Street, St Nicholas Street and Queen Street. In May of the same year the route was completed along Felixstowe Road as far as the Royal Oak, although an interim service had been provided as far as Duke Street as installations progressed. After this there was no further route development.

The advent of the 1914-1918 War created some severe difficulties for the undertaking. Many employees were required for war service, which led to staff shortages, and this resulted in the employment of women as conductresses. A lack of steel and spare parts made it difficult to maintain both vehicles and infrastructure, particularly the track. The latter was affected by the heavy wartime traffic through the town and in 1917 the track in the Bath Street branch was lifted for use elsewhere and never replaced. A lack of paint resulted in a number of trams being painted in grey.

In the post war period some track was renewed in 1921 when steel supplies improved and short sections doubled. However the Tramway Department was faced with the capital cost of renewal to track and road surfaces, which were in a poor state of repair.

Following the resignation of the General Manager Mr F Ayton, and the appointment of a new manager Mr A S Black in 1921, thoughts turned to the possible use of "trackless trams" i.e. trolleybuses. It was decided to construct an experimental route by converting the section between Cornhill and the Station; this was also the opening route of the horse tram system. Three Railless single deck trolleybuses were hired and the service commenced on 2nd September 1923 with connections to the tram services at the Cornhill.

The experiment was successful but arguments followed as to whether the trams should be replaced by trolleybuses or motorbuses. A further complication arose when the Eastern Counties Road Car Company offered to operate replacement motorbuses and acquire the tramway system plus the three trolleybuses.

All of this resulted in the Corporation carrying out a referendum of ratepayers as to whether they should proceed to promote a Parliamentary Bill to operate trolleybuses on all routes. The outcome was 3,780 in favour and 2,156 against resulting in the Ipswich Corporation Act receiving Royal Assent on 7th August 1925.

Two further experimental trolleybuses were purchased, namely a Ransomes Sims & Jefferies (RS&J) in 1924 and a Tilling-Stevens in 1925. To open the tramway replacement programme thirty single deck trolleybuses were delivered, equally split between RS&J and Garrett. The next route to be converted was between Cornhill and Bourne Bridge (Wherstead Road) on 17th July 1925; this was before the Act had completed the parliamentary process. The original tram route had been disrupted during the construction of the new Stoke Bridge over the River Orwell.

Conversions to trolleybuses quickly followed with Felixstowe Road on 27th May 1926 (extended to Kings Way), Lattice Barn and Derby Road Station on 9th June 1926 and the remaining Norwich and Bramford Roads (with the latter extended to Adair Road) on 27th July 1926; the last day of tram operation was the preceding day. Six trams, plus one body, were sold to Scarborough Tramways; the bodies of many of the others were used as sheds locally.

As indicated earlier, Ipswich was one of the first United Kingdom systems to change from trams to trolleybuses but the electric trams had only a short life of just less than 23 years. Their demise in 1926 ended over 45 years of railed street public transport in the town. Whilst the electric trams had only lasted nearly 23 years electric traction would continue for a further 37 years with the introduction of the replacing trolleybuses.

ORIGINAL ELECTRIC TRAM ROUTES AND NIGHT LAMP HEADCODES

Ipswich Railway Station – Cornhill Shuttle
Felixstowe Road – Cornhill – Bourne Bridge)
Bramford Road – Cornhill – Lattice Barn) Connecting cross town services
Whitton – Cornhill – Derby Road Station)

Felixstowe Road and Wherstead Road.	Whitton and Derby Road.	Cornhill and Railway Station.	Bramford Road and Lattice Barn.

LATER ELECTRIC TRAM ROUTES WITH COLOURED ROUTE NUMBERS

1 Green Whitton – Cornhill – Bourne Bridge
2 White Bramford Road – Cornhill – Derby Road Station
3 Blue Ipswich Railway Station – Cornhill – Lattice Barn
4 Red Ipswich Railway Station – Cornhill – Felixstowe Road

The above are as per the map.
Route numbers were introduced circa 1922 with destinations displayed on the dash.

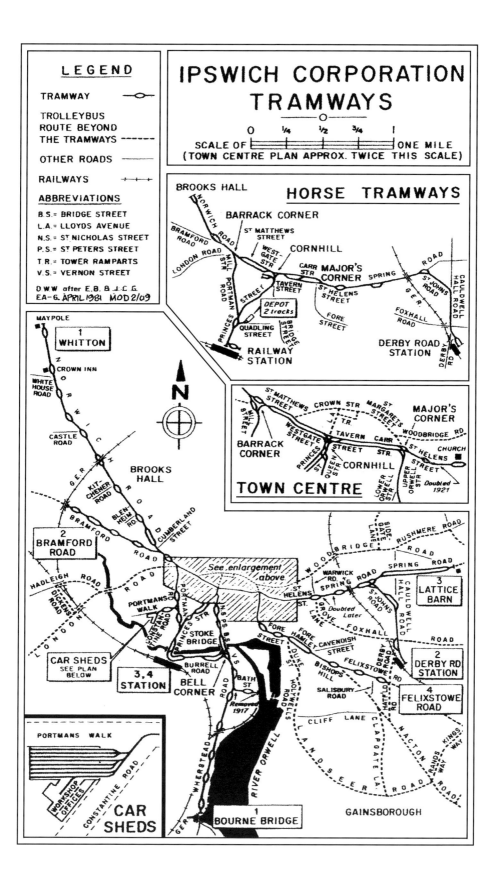

IPSWICH CORPORATION TRAMWAYS

LEGEND

TRAMWAY

TROLLEYBUS ROUTE BEYOND THE TRAMWAYS

OTHER ROADS

RAILWAYS

ABBREVIATIONS

B.S.= BRIDGE STREET
L.A.= LLOYDS AVENUE
N.S.= St NICHOLAS STREET
P.S.= St PETERS STREET
T.R.= TOWER RAMPARTS
V.S.= VERNON STREET

D.W.W. after E.B. B. J.C.G.
EA-6. APRIL 1981 MOD 2/09

SCALE OF
0   1/4   1/2   3/4   ONE MILE
(TOWN CENTRE PLAN APPROX. TWICE THIS SCALE)

HORSE TRAMWAYS

BROOKS HALL
BARRACK CORNER
St MATTHEWS STREET
NORWICH ROAD
BRAMFORD ROAD
CORNHILL
WEST-GATE STR
LONDON ROAD
MILL STR
PORTMAN ROAD
PRINCES STREET
CARR STR
MAJOR'S CORNER
TAVERN STREET
St HELENS STREET
SPRING ROAD
St JOHNS ROAD
CAULDWELL HALL ROAD
DEPOT 2 tracks
QUADLING STREET
BRIDGE STREET
FORE STREET
FOXHALL ROAD
RAILWAY STATION
DERBY ROAD STATION
DERBY RD

TOWN CENTRE

St MATTHEWS STREET
CROWN STR
St MARGARETS STREET
MAJOR'S CORNER
MILL STREET
T.R.
WOODBRIDGE RD
BARRACK CORNER
WESTGATE STREET
TAVERN STREET
CARR STR
St HELENS STREET
CHURCH
PRINCES ST
QUEEN ST
CORNHILL
UPPER ORWELL STR
LOWER ORWELL ST
Doubled 1921

MAYPOLE

1 WHITTON

CROWN INN
WHITE HOUSE ROAD
NORWICH ROAD
CASTLE ROAD
BROOKS HALL
KITCHENER ROAD
BLENHEIM RD
BRAMFORD ROAD
CUMBERLAND STREET
GER

2 BRAMFORD ROAD

HADLEIGH ROAD
DICKENS ROAD
LONDON ROAD
CONSTANTINE ROAD
PORTMANS WALK
PORTMAN STR
PRINCES STR
N.S. P.S. B.S. V.S.
See enlargement above
WARWICK RD.
SPRING ROAD
St HELENS ST.
WOODBRIDGE ROAD
SIDEGATE LANE
RUSHMERE ROAD
SPRING ROAD
St JOHNS ROAD
CAULDWELL HALL ROAD

3 LATTICE BARN

GROVE LANE
Doubled Later
FOXHALL ROAD
STOKE BRIDGE
BURRELL ROAD
BELL CORNER
BATH ST
Removed 1917
FORE STREET
FORE STREET
HAMLET ROAD
CAVENDISH STREET
DUKE ST
BISHOPS HILL
FELIXSTOWE RD
DERBY RD
HATFIELD RD

3,4 STATION

2 DERBY RD STATION

SALISBURY ROAD

4 FELIXSTOWE ROAD

CAR SHEDS SEE PLAN BELOW

CLIFF LANE
CLAPGATE LA.
NACTON ROAD
LANDSEER ROAD
RANDS WAY
KINGS WAY
HOLYWELLS ROAD
WHERSTEAD ROAD
RIVER ORWELL

CAR SHEDS

PORTMANS WALK
WORKSHOP
OFFICES
CONSTANTINE ROAD

1 BOURNE BRIDGE

GAINSBOROUGH

TOWN CENTRE
Cornhill

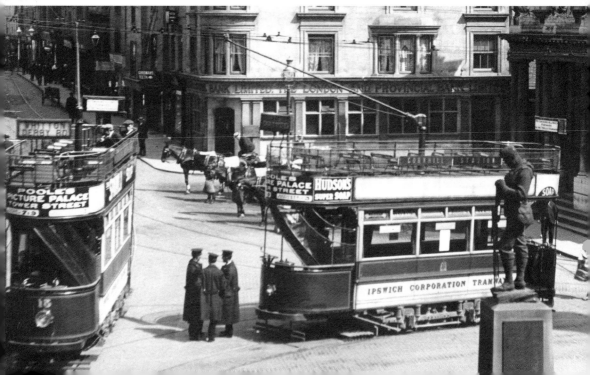

← 1. The Cornhill was the hub of the Ipswich tramway system as depicted in the next series of pictures. In this scene three trams are in view with the then Post Office building on the right. On the left Car 33 enters Cornhill from Tavern Street on its way to Whitton having passed Car 18 moving away in the opposite direction destined for Felixstowe Road. In the foreground Car 23 waits to make the return trip to the Station via Princes Street and will leave to the right of the Post Office. (Author's postcard)

← 2. A triangular junction was formed in the Cornhill with all routes using this hub. In this post 1909 view Car 15 on the left is destined for Whitton having travelled from Derby Road Station. A staff conference is taking place next to an unidentified car waiting to depart along Princes Street to Ipswich Station with the route indicator board mounted on the upper deck protective guarding. (Author's postcard)

3.　　　Lattice Barn is the destination of Car 28 as it prepares to leave Cornhill and enter Tavern Street and follow the sister vehicle in the background. The advertisement for Royal Blue House boots on the roof of the property on the right must have been difficult to apply and of doubtful benefit. (Author's postcard)

FROM CORNHILL TO IPSWICH STATION.

WEEK DAYS.					SUNDAYS.										
7 5	10 24	1 36	4 48	8 8	p.m.	6 0	8 0	8 42	11 54	3 6	6 18	10 17	3 45	7 30	9 30
7 17	10 30	1 42	4 54	8 16	12 15	6 6	8 6	8 48	12 0	3 1	6 24	10 31	4 0	7 39	9 36
7 29	10 36	1 48	5 0	8 24	12 30	6 12	8 12	8 54	12 6	3 18	6 30	10 47	4 15	7 42	9 42
7 33	10 42	1 54	5 6	8 33	12 45	6 18	8 18	9 0	12 12	3 24	6 36	10 56	4 30	7 48	9 48
7 40	10 48	2 0	5 12	8 40	1 0	6 24	8 24	9 6	12 18	3 30	6 42		4 45	7 54	9 54
7 46	10 54	2 6	5 18	8 48	1 15	6 30	8 30	9 12	12 24	3 36	6 48		5 0		10 0
7 50	11 0	2 12	5 24	8 56	1 30	6 36	8 38	9 18	12 30	3 42	6 54		5 15		10 6
7 55	11 6	2 18	5 30	9 4	1 45	6 42	8 42	9 24	12 36	3 48	7 0		5 30		10 12
8 0	11 12	2 24	5 36	9 12	2 0	6 48	8 48	9 30	12 42	3 54	7 6		5 45		10 18
8 6	11 18	2 30	5 42	9 20	2 15	6 54	8 54	9 36	12 48	4 0	7 10		5 58		10 24
8 12	11 24	2 36	5 48	9 28	2 30	7 0	9 0	9 42	12 54	4 6	7 14				10 32
8 18	11 30	2 42	5 54	9 36	2 45	7 6	9 6	9 48	1 0	4 12	7 22				
8 25	11 36	2 48	6 0	9 44	3 0	7 12	9 12	9 54	1 6	4 18	7 30				
8 32	11 42	2 54	6 6	9 52	3 15	7 18	9 18	10 0	1 12	4 24	7 38				
8 39	11 48	3 0	6 12	10 6	3 30	7 24	9 24	10 6	1 18	4 30	7 46				
								10 12	1 24	4 36	7 54				
								10 18	1 30	4 42	8 0				

4.   A 1890's view of Cornhill showing an open top horse tram with knifeboard upper deck seating. A junction leading to double track can be seen in Tavern Street just above the cabby's hut; the latter was moved to Christchurch Park in later years. The shop of Bales the gun maker has a wide variety of sporting supplies advertised including billiards, golf, fishing, cricket and tennis. (Author's postcard)

5.   With the London and Provincial Bank in the background Car 36 waits on layover whilst working the Cornhill-Station shuttle; the crew appear to be taking their break on the top deck. This view was probably taken during the 1914-1918 war, or just afterwards, as the car appears to be in grey livery and side panelling is missing presumably because of a shortage of materials and/or skilled labour. (Author's postcard)

6.   The Bath Street branch was mentioned in the opening section on the system history. Here an unidentified car waits in Cornhill before departing to this destination. The car will carry the passengers to the River Orwell berths for the paddle steamers that plied down the river to Felixstowe, Harwich and beyond. Three vessels were operated by the Great Eastern Railway and were named *Norfolk*, *Suffolk* and *Essex* (see Pictures 65 and 66). The destination blind on the car indicates "Steamers". (Author's postcard)

7.   Car 16 sweeps round the eastern side of the Cornhill triangle with a full load on its way to Wherstead Road Railway Bridge, a short working of the Bourne Bridge route, on what appears to be a warm sunny day. The car has travelled from Felixstowe Road and passed the turreted building in the background that housed the Picture House cinema. (Author's postcard)

➔   8. There was traffic congestion even in the early 1900s! In this view of the Cornhill three unidentified trams are in view; the left hand one is destined for Derby Road Station and the right hand tram will leave via Princes Street for the Station or Bourne Bridge. A Great Eastern Railway delivery wagon has centre stage being drawn by what may be two Suffolk Punch horses under the control of a bowler-hatted drayman. (Author's postcard)

➔   9. A further view of a horse tram in Cornhill with the company title above the lower deck windows and upper deck passengers residing on back to back knifeboard seating. (Author's collection)

10.   In this pre 1903 Cornhill view one of the tramway company's horse trams can be seen but with competition on the scene in the form of a horse bus of the Ipswich Omnibus Service (see Picture 42).   Notwithstanding the advent of mass public transport plenty of cabbies are available for hire, parked on the former site of the cabby's hut (see Picture 4). Note the stub parking track in the foreground. (Ipswich Transport Museum)

IPSWICH TRAMWAYS

FIRST DAYS' RECEIPTS

The Ipswich electric tramcars continue to excite considerable interest among the inhabitants, and there has been almost continuously since Monday morning a large crowd on the Cornhill, who have gazed collectively on the passing cars with unvarying interest mingled with wonder. On Monday there were 12 cars out during the early part of the day, and afterwards two specials were added, and the same programme was observed on Tuesday. The number of passengers who paid fares on Monday was nearly 14,000 and the cash receipts about £66. On Tuesday evening there was an unfortunate hiatus in the supply of electricity and for nearly an hour the cars wherever they were at the time resembled the bewitched persons in the fairy tale who were put to sleep for a period. Later in the evening they were running again in all the glory of electric light, and were well patronised on all the town portions of the route.

11.	This view of Cornhill is taken from the junction of Princes Street (centre) and Queen Street (to the right) and has three unidentified cars on the sides of the triangular junction with the insurance company buildings towering in the background. Trams going to Bourne Bridge used the Queen Street track curving to the right. (Author's postcard)

12.	A view from the eastern side of Cornhill, and looking along Westgate Street, depicts Car 1 being prepared for a return trip to the Station. The conductor is on the upper deck to swing the seat backs over so passengers are facing in a forward direction. Grimwade's clothing shop forms the backdrop and in the foreground an imposing gas lamp stands amongst the cabby's parking lot. (Author's postcard)

13.   This further pre 1903 view depicts a fully laden double deck horse tram which will no doubt tax the strength of the two horses on the initial start. The upper deck knifeboard seating is again well illustrated and even at this early period a policeman is on duty standing by the side of the tram. The celebratory flags may be to commemorate Queen Victoria's Diamond Jubilee in 1897. (Author's postcard)

➜   14. An early motorcar overtakes Car 17 destined for Lattice Barn, having travelled from Bramford Road; a black on white destination indicator is fitted. The limited space between the outside rails of the double track and the kerb, a feature of the town centre layouts, is well illustrated when looking along Westgate Street. Grimwade's summer clearance sale is well advertised. (Author's postcard)

➜   15. At the same location Car 35 awaits departure to Derby Road Station having arrived from the Whitton direction, although the destination blind shows Norwich Road again on a white background; this may be a short working of the Whitton route. The curved track on the left led into Princes Street and the Lloyd's building can be seen on the right.
(Author's postcard)

16.	On the western side of the triangular junction in ➔ 17. Also on the western side an unidentified car is seen in profile circa 1904 positioned to enter Princes Street on the right. The premises of Bales the gun maker seen in Picture 4 has now been occupied by Palmer, the London tailor. (Author's postcard)

16.	On the western side of the triangular junction in Cornhill Car 4 stands waiting to depart to the Great Eastern Railway (GER) river steamer berths at the end of Bath Street or to pick up workers from the Ransomes and Rapier factory; it will travel via the Railway Station and Burrell Road. This view was taken in late 1903 or 1904 as there are no side destination boards on the upper deck. (Author's postcard)

➔ 18. Car 27 leaves Cornhill and is about to enter Westgate Street. The policeman on point duty illustrates the increase in traffic that has occurred at this central point of Ipswich. To his right is an Ipswich Sanitary Authority wagon standing next to buildings occupied by a number of insurance companies. (Author's postcard)

TO LATTICE BARN/DERBY ROAD STATION/ FELIXSTOWE ROAD

Tavern Street/Carr Street/Majors Corner

19.   Car 8 moves along Tavern Street on its way to Derby Road Station in the early 1900's and is just about to pass under a section insulator/feeder. It appears to be a warm day with the lady under the H Samuel shop sunblind having raised her parasol. Also note the numerous light bulbs on the upper H Samuel signage. (Author's postcard)

20.   A well patronised horse tram makes its way along Tavern Street with the White Horse Hotel on the left in the far distance. The decorations probably commemorated the 1897 Diamond Jubilee. The telegram boy on the right seems interested in the young female on the opposite side of the road. (Ipswich Transport Museum)

21.   Car 31 moves along Tavern Street towards Cornhill with the horse drawn cab moving across to the left to allow the tram to pass. Next to the H Samuel shop is the Picture House Cinema, which is now the site of the Boots outlet. (Author's postcard)

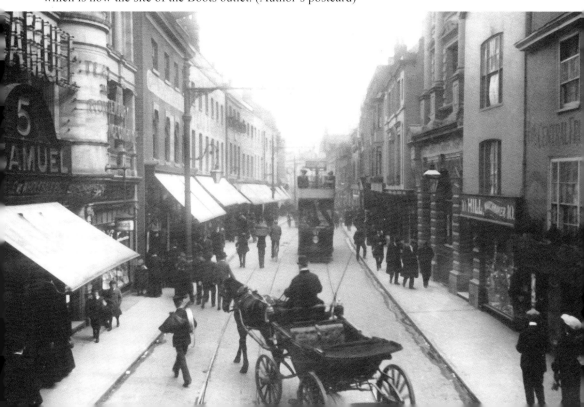

22. This view looking along Tavern Street towards Cornhill again emphasises the narrowness of the town centre streets. An unidentified tramcar can be seen in the distance followed by an early motorcar, with the entrance to the White Horse Hotel in the right foreground. Note the stop sign above the smartly dressed boy. (Author's postcard)

IPSWICH TRAMWAYS.

Tramway receipts for week ending Nov. 16th, 1907, are as follows:—

	£	s.	d.
Sunday	33	7	5½
Monday	40	2	2¼
Tuesday	45	2	8½
Wednesday	47	1	2
Thursday	43	12	5½
Friday	42	12	7
Saturday	58	17	3
	£310	15	10

Average per car mile, 6.41.
Car miles, 11,627.
No. of passengers, 79,250.

Corresponding week last year, £351 19s.0 ½d.
Average per car mile, 7.06.

23.　This view, looking along Tavern Street from its junction with Northgate Street, has Car 7 approaching the White Horse Hotel on the right; this hostelry figured in Charles Dickens' "Pickwick Papers". The traction standard on the right has the stop sign seen in the previous picture indicating "All cars from town stop here". (Burrows collection, Newham Museum; commercial postcard)

24.　This view along Carr Street, looking from the junction with Northgate Street, illustrates well the narrowness of the central streets where a horse drawn vehicle, with one set of wheels in the tram track, passes an unidentified car destined for Norwich Road. The gap between the outside rails and the pavement kerb is again minimal; a single track in the centre of the road would not have left sufficient passing space on either side of the tram. An early motorcar can be seen to the rear. (Author's postcard)

25.　　Car 17 rounds the bend at the end of Carr Street in the early 1920s as it moves towards Majors Corner. The entrance to the Lyceum Theatre is on the extreme left and next to it is a sign of the changing times indicated by the advent of motor garage premises. For some reason one of the traction standards carrying the overhead has had the lower section painted in a lighter colour. (Author's postcard)

→　26.　An unidentified car has just left Majors Corner and moves along Carr Street on its way to Cornhill in 1908 with the destination indicator showing "Special Car". On the left is the building that housed The Bee Hive public house, although it is vacant here, and immediately beyond are the premises of W. Howard, sanitary and hot water engineer. In the foreground tram tracks lead off to the left into Upper Orwell Street, whilst those on the right enter St Helens Street. (Author's collection)

→　27.　This view indicates the track layout at Majors Corner, with St Helens Street in the foreground, Upper Orwell Street lower left and the track from the town centre along Carr Street leading into the junction next to the antiques shop. The curve into Upper Orwell Street was extremely tight at 40ft (12.2m) radius. (Author's postcard)

St Helens Street/Spring Road

28.   Car 6 leaves Majors Corner and is about to enter single track in St. Helens Street on its way to Lattice Barn having travelled from Bramford Road. This is in the early years of the system with black on white destination blind and when the buildings on the left were private residences, including that of the Major family (hence Majors Corner), with rear gardens that stretched through to Woodbridge Road. In the background is County Hall, the offices of Suffolk County Council until their recent move to more modern accommodation at Endeavour House.
(Ipswich Transport Museum)

➔   29. Car 14 has just entered St Helens Street from Majors Corner with the antiques shop seen in Picture 27 immediately behind the tram. On the right is an advertisement for the Lyceum Theatre publicising "The Marriage of Kitty".
(David Kindred collection)

➔   30. Almost at the same location, but looking in the opposite direction, Car 24 is seen post 1922 when route numbers were introduced. The buildings on the left have made way for garage/ workshop facilities belonging to Botwoods Ltd. County Hall is again in view and the majority of the buildings on the right still exist. (Ipswich Transport Museum)

31.   Further along St. Helens Street Car 23 traverses the passing loop early in the life of the system; it is minus a destination blind. This section of track from Majors Corner to Orchard Street was doubled after the 1914-18 War. On the left is the corner of Regent Street. The column in the foreground is a telegraph pole. (Author's collection)

→   32. Cars 18 and 24, both carrying the same advertisements, pass each other in St Helens Street near the Warwick Road/Grove Lane junction. On the right is a feeder box supplying power to the overhead section insulator carried by the bracket arm. Mounted on the traction standard are two stop signs, one indicating "All cars from town stop here" and the other "Tramway fare stage". Typical Victorian pallisaded houses complete the picture with Frank Norse's coal delivery cart in the foreground. (Author's postcard)

→   33. Car 13 and 22 are seen in the passing loop against the background of the impressive viaduct that carried the railway line from Ipswich to Derby Road Station and onwards to Felixstowe. Note the paved area each side of the track, which was the tram department's responsibility. (Author's postcard)

FROM LATTICE BARN
To CORNHILL & NORWICH RD. BRIDGE

WEEK DAYS.			SUNDAYS.	
a.m.	p.m.	p.m.	p.m.	p.m.
†7 4	1 10	7 10	12 29	7 10
7 19	1 22	7 22	12 44	7 22
7 27	1 34	7 34	12 59	7 34
7 37	1 46	7 46	1 14	7 46
7 43	1 58	7 58	1 22	7 58
8 4	2 10	8 10	1 34	8 10
8 13	2 22	8 22	1 46	8 22
8 25	2 34	8 34	1 58	8 34
8 35	2 46	8 46	2 10	8 46
8 46	2 58	8 58	2 22	8 58
8 58	3 10	9 10	2 34	9 10
9 11	3 22	9 22	2 46	9 22
9 23	3 34	9 34	2 58	9 34
9 34	3 46	9 46	3 10	9 46

9 46	3 58	9 58	3 22	*9 58
9 58	4 10	10 10	3 34	10*10
10 10	4 22	10 22	3 46	10*20
10 22	4 34	10*34	3 58	
10 34	4 46	10*46	4 10	
10 46	4 58		4 22	
10 58	5 10		4 34	
11 10	5 22		4 46	
11 22	5 34		4 58	
11 34	5 46		5 10	
11 46	5 58		5 22	
11 58	6 10		5 34	
p.m.	6 22		5 46	
12 10	6 34		5 58	
12 22	6 46		6 10	
12 34	6 58		6 22	
12 46			6 34	
12 58			6 46	
			6 58	

*To Cornhill only   Route 8—BLUE Light

34.   Car 10 is seen at the junction of Spring Road and St Johns Road, with the latter to the right. After this junction Spring Road rises sharply to Cauldwell Hall Road. The view well illustrates the reverse staircase, which did not provide much headroom for the motorman. The car will continue along the full length of Spring Road to Lattice Barn. (Author's postcard)

35.   At the brow of the hill at the junction with Cauldwell Hall Road the double track curves onto the level section leading to Lattice Barn, the name of a public house situated where Spring Road joins Woodbridge Road. An inward bound car approaches buildings that are little changed today, although the road junction is now controlled by traffic lights.
(National Tramway Museum; commercial postcard)

St Johns Road/Cauldwell Hall Road/Derby Road Station

36.   At the junction of Spring Road and St Johns Road three cars meet circa 1904. In the foreground two unidentified cars have just passed each other on the St Johns Road tracks, whilst in the background Car 25 drops down Spring Road towards the town centre. (Author's postcard)

TRAMWAY WIRE MISHAP.

An overhead tramway wire snapped on Wednesday morning, in St. Helen's street, Ipswich, and falling to the ground, caused a lot of brilliant electric flashes.   Fortunately the falling of the wire was unattended with serious consequences, though it is stated one or two passers-by at the time had narrow escapes from coming into contact with the wire.   The traffic was promptly stopped for a while in the vicinity of the accident, and the damage repaired by a break-down gang from the tramway station.

IPSWICH   CORPORATION TRAMWAYS

RELEASE OF CERTAIN EMPLOYEES FOR
WAR SERVICE
and
EMPLOYMENT OF WOMEN AS
TEMPORARY CONDUCTORS

The Electric Supply and Tramways Committee have arranged to release a number of Conductors in order that the latter, as soon as their places can be filled, may be employed in the production of Munitions of War, the undersigned will be pleased to receive offers of service as temporary Tramway Conductors for the period of the War, or such shorter period as may be necessary, from women above 21 years of age.   They will be paid the commencing wage given to male Conductors of full age, namely, at the rate of 22s per average week of 60 hours, 10 hours per day.   Sunday duties are worked in rotation.   Uniform overalls and hats will be provided.

Owing to the nature of the employment, applications can only be considered from women of good physique and strong constitution.

Offers of service should be made, in the first instance, in writing, stating age, approximate height and nature of previous employment, if any.

F. AYTON
Chief Engineer and Manager,
Electric Supply and Tramways Department,
Constantine Road.
13th May 1915

37.	St Johns Road climbs from its junction with Spring Road up to Cauldwell Hall Road. An unidentified car drops down the hill under overhead supported by bracket arms. The majority of the houses have cast iron railings in front of their small gardens; the former were removed during the Second World War to provide much needed raw material.
(National Tramway Museum; commercial postcard)

IPSWICH CORPORATION TRAMWAYS

SPECIAL SERVICE OF CARS TO
DERBY ROAD STATION

BEGINNING on MONDAY the 2nd May in ADDITION to the Ordinary Service at present running. SPECIAL CARS will leave CORNHILL for DERBY ROAD STATION daily on connection with the Train Service to Felixstowe at 8.10, 8.55, 10.5, 11.45am, and 1.5, 3.5, 4.40, 5.15, 6.5, 6.40, and 7.30pm. And FROM Derby Road Station on the arrival of all trains from Felixstowe.

FRANK AYTON
Chief Engineer and Manager
28th April 1904

FROM DERBY RD. STATION
To CORNHILL & BRAMFORD RD. TERM

WEEK DAYS.				SUNDAYS.	
a.m.	p.m.	p.m.	p.m.	p.m.	p.m.
7 10	12 6	6 6	12 15	7 6	
7 28	12 18	6 18	12 30	7 18	
7 40	12 30	6 30	12 41	7 30	
7 50	12 42	6 42	12 56	7 42	
8 0	12 54	6 54	1 11	7 54	
8 10	*1 0	7 6	1 26	8 6	
8 21	1 6	7 18	1 41	8 18	
8 30	1 18	7 30	1 54	8 30	
8 42	1 30	7 42	2 6	8 42	
8 54	1 42	7 54	2 18	8 54	
9 6	1 54	8 6	2 30	9 6	
9 18	2 6	8 18	2 42	9 18	
9 30	2 18	8 30	2 54	9 30	
9 42	2 30	8 42	3 6	9 42	
9 54	2 42	8 54	3 18	9 50	
10 6	2 54	9 6	3 30	10 2*	
10 18	3 6	9 18	3 42	10 14*	
10 30	3 18	9 30	3 54		
10 42	3 30	9 42	4 6		
10 54	3 42	9 54	4 18		
11 6	3 54	10 6	4 30		
11 18	4 6	10 18	4 42		
11 30	4 18	10 30*	4 54		
11 42	4 30	10 42*	5 6		
11 54	4 42	10 45*	5 18		
	4 54		5 30		
	5 6		5 42		
	5 18		5 54		
	5 30		6 6		
	5 42		6 18		
	5 54		6 30		
			6 42		
			6 54		

*Barrack Corner   R 19th   -W ALCL C.G.H.

38.   At the top of St Johns Road the tracks turn into Cauldwell Hall Road and thence to Derby Road and the station. Cars 14 and 24 make their way on the outward journey whilst Car 7 returns to Cornhill and onwards to Whitton circa 1904.
(Author's postcard)

39.   Car 35 approaches the end of the line and the entrance to Derby Road Station, which is to the immediate right of the boy carrying the basket. In the background is the Railway Hotel on Foxhall Road and to the extreme left is Cauldwell Hall Road leading to the top of St Johns Road. When the horse tramway was opened early routes were to the East and West of the town centre with no connection between the two until later. In these early days the eastern horse trams were housed adjacent to the Railway Hotel. (Author's collection)

40.   The tram track ran from the road to terminate in the Derby Road Station yard and here Car 25 poses for an official photograph at that location circa 1904/05. This arrangement was very beneficial when dealing with passengers participating in rail excursions. The uniformed inspector on the right is perhaps training a newly recruited conductor since the latter appears to still be in civilian clothing. (Ipswich Transport Museum)

➔   41. At the same location a horse tram, possibly rebuilt from a single deck car, is seen with supporting cast. The bowler hatted driver stands with his hand on the brake whilst also holding a whip; the conductor stands close by. The upper deck females are looking down on the male group with the second person from the left appearing to be a railway employee. (Ipswich Transport Museum)

➔   42. Here is an example of the competition that the horse tramway company faced from 1898 in the form of the Ipswich Omnibus Service. This company, with it's red painted horse buses, opened up a number of services in competition with the horse trams which led to a fares war. The omnibus company ceased to provide services after the introduction of electric trams by the Corporation. The picture has been included here, given the side indicator board that shows Derby Road as a destination, with a one penny fare from Cornhill. A two pence fare from Cornhill to the Ostrich public house beyond Bourne Bridge on Wherstead Road is also advertised. Note the rear wheel brake pad. (Ipswich Transport Museum)

Fore Street/Fore Hamlet

43. This rather poor view has been included as it is the only photograph located that depicts a tram in this part of Fore Street. A Car, possibly 18, is seen near the junction with Grimwade Street, previously known as Church Street, circa 1904. (D Kindred collection)

➜ 44. Car 18 is about to leave Fore Street and enter Fore Hamlet on its way to Felixstowe Road before beginning the climb up Bishops Hill. On the left is the Social Settlement building that was opened in 1896 as a non-political and non-denominational community to give support to poor and needy families before the days of the welfare state. Beyond the tram is the Earl Grey public house; both buildings were demolished to make way for road improvement schemes. (Author's postcard)

➜ 45. To the right of Car 18 in the previous picture is Duke Street. As the Felixstowe Road route was being constructed trams ran as far as Duke Street when the first stage of the line was completed. Also housed in Duke Street was an electricity sub station and the inside is illustrated here; the person in short sleeves was Robert Gooch. The tramway connection is that the Electricity Supply and Tramway departments were operated as a single integrated unit under one manager; this sub station did not supply the trams but provided power to this area of the town. (Author's postcard)

46.   Another view of the Social Settlement building taken from the opposite direction with Car 21 waiting for boarding passengers before departing for Wherstead Road via Stoke Bridge. (Ipswich Transport Museum)

IPSWICH CORPORATION TRAMWAYS.

NOTICE.

Opening of Route to Felixstowe Road Terminus

ON and AFTER WEDNESDAY, the 18th May, there will be a THROUGH SERVICE of CARS between BOURNE BRIDGE and FELIXSTOWE ROAD TERMINUS.

CARS will run EVERY TEN MINUTES, and Time Tables may be seen on the Notice Boards at each Terminus, and also at the Cornhill.

Cars will start from Felixstowe Road Terminus at the hour and every ten minutes, and from Bourne Bridge at five minutes past the hour, and every ten minutes.

Bishops Hill/Felixstowe Road

47.   Car 15 descends Bishops Hill and passes the end of Myrtle Road before entering Fore Hamlet on its way to Wherstead Road. Note the gas lamp over the doorway of George Cox's butchers shop (shipping supplied) and the coal delivery wagon on the left. (Author's postcard)

48.   Car 7 climbs Bishops Hill on single track to reach Felixstowe Road; this was the steepest incline on the system. The young lad appears to be resting on his handcart either out of exhaustion after climbing the hill or to allow the photographer to take his picture. This section of the road was widened in later years. (Author's postcard)

49.   Car 9 has just climbed Bishops Hill, and is about to pass under an overhead feeder/section insulator as it enters a deserted Felixstowe Road, having travelled from Wherstead Road (Bourne Bridge).
(Author's postcard)

From FELIXSTOWE ROAD to CORNHILL

WEEK DAYS.					SUNDAYS.		
a.m.	a.m.	p.m.	p.m.	p.m.	p.m.	p.m.	p.m.
6 47	10 34	1 58	5 34	9 10	12 34	4 10	7 46
7 15	10 46	2 10	5 46	9 22	12 46	4 22	7 58
7 25	10 58	2 22	5 58	9 34	12 58	4 34	8 10
7 35	11 10	2 34	6 10	9 46	1 10	4 46	8 22
7 46	11 22	2 46	6 22	9 58	1 22	4 58	8 34
7 58	11 34	2 58	6 34	10 10	1 34	5 10	8 46
8 10	11 46	3 10	6 46	10 22	1 46	5 22	8 58
8 22	11 58	3 22	6 58	10 34	1 58	5 34	9 10
8 34	p.m.	3 34	7 10	10 42	2 10	5 46	9 22
8 46	12 10	3 46	7 22		2 22	5 58	9 34
8 58	12 22	3 58	7 34		2 34	6 10	9 46
9 10	12 34	4 10	7 46		2 46	6 22	9 58
9 22	12 46	4 22	7 58		2 58	6 34	10 5
9 34	12 58	4 34	8 10		3 10	6 46	10 17
9 46	1 10	4 46	8 22		3 22	6 58	
9 58	1 22	4 58	8 34		3 34	7 10	
10 10	1 34	5 10	8 46		3 46	7 22	
10 23	1 46	5 22	8 58		3 58	7 34	

Route 4—RED Light.

50.   The end of the line of the Felixstowe Road route is depicted here with the Royal Oak public house and Derby Road on the right. Car 21 waits to depart to Wherstead Road via Stoke Bridge as the group of lads on the left watch the photographer's activities. (Author's postcard)

51.   A later view, taken in the early 1920's, of the Felixstowe Road terminus with Car 28 waiting to return to town. A route number box has now been installed in lieu of a destination indicator and a fare stage sign is mounted on the left hand traction standard. (Ipswich Transport Museum)

52.　　Car 17 is seen here at the Felixstowe Road terminus at the junction with Derby and Hatfield Roads and with the Royal Oak public house in the background. The route indicator board can be seen mounted on the upper deck guarding and with a front advertisement for Poole's Picture Palace situated in Tower Street, which provided twice nightly performances at 7 and 9.
(D Kindred collection)

TO WHERSTEAD ROAD
(BOURNE BRIDGE)

Queen Street/
St Nicholas Street/
St Peters Street

53. This view shows the S bend in the tracks being laid at the top of Queen Street which joins that in Princes Street where the workmen are standing. The building on the right currently houses Barclays Bank. (Author's collection)

> **TRAMCAR OFF THE LINE AT IPSWICH**
>
> About 3.30 on Monday afternoon one section of the Ipswich tram service was for some time temporarily disorganised by one of the cars running on the Wherstead Road route leaving the metals at the points just below the Princes Street entrance to the Corn Exchange. As everyone knows, the curve at the entrance to Queen Street is extremely sharp; whether or not the curving was responsible for the mishap cannot be determined – more probably it was due to clogging of the points. The car, which was travelling at a slow rate of speed, ran some 20 yards or more after leaving the metals, cutting into the wooden pavement considerably; it was drawn onto the metals again by another car from the Cornhill. The long expected change at the formation of the line at this spot is still delayed – perhaps this mishap may have the effect of directing public attention to the matter. 26th September 1905

54. Car 31 has left Queen Street and now moves along St Nicholas Street towards St Peters Street on its way to Wherstead Road around 1906. The narrowness of the town centre streets is again well illustrated. The railings on the left mark the site of the St Nicholas Congregational Church that was demolished in 1968. (Commercial postcard)

55.　　In this circa 1904 view Car 8 is about to leave St Nicholas Street and enter St Peters Street with Silent Street on the right. It is suggested that Cardinal Wolsey was born amongst the old buildings illustrated and the pharmacy on the corner has taken full advantage of this idea. Note the pharmacy offers the facility of a dark room. Although most of the town centre used bracket arms to carry the overhead wiring, span wires have been used here.
(Author's postcard)

IPSWICH CORPORATION TRAMWAYS

IMPORTANT NOTICE.

IT has been decided to CONTINUE the TEN MINUTES' (SUMMER) TRAMWAY SERVICE THROUGH THE PRESENT MONTH. The running times set forth in the September Time Tables, and not those printed in the October Time Tables, will therefore apply.

TO-DAY (SATURDAY) the ordinary Ten Minutes' Service is being run in place of the emergency service, necessitated by the shortage of electric power.

The Electric Power Station is now able to supply all demands.

By order of the Electric Supply and Tramways Committee.

F. AYTON,
Chief Engineer and Manager.
October 1st, 1920.

56.   A view taken circa 1904/05 at the same location depicts Car 28 moving in the opposite direction on its way to Felixstowe Road. (Author's postcard)

57.   The newsagents' premises of T H Palmer at 33-35 St Nicholas Street frame this view of an unidentified car leaving St Peters Street. The tower of St Peters church dominates the skyline and the building on the right is the Hippodrome Theatre that was demolished in 1985.
(Author's postcard)

58.　　With St Peters Church as a backdrop Car 21 moves along St Peters Street on its way to Felixstowe Road having crossed Stoke Bridge just out of view on the right. The properties on the left are little changed today, although the businesses now trading from them would probably be a surprise to the Edwardians. (Author's collection)

Bridge Street/Stoke Bridge/Vernon Street

59.   The next two views show the railway crossing in Bridge Street, adjacent to Stoke Bridge, which ran between the Commercial Road sidings on the left and the St Peters Port quayside. A rail crossing still exists today but it is unused, although all the appropriate warning signs are on display. This view looks towards the town centre with the tower of St Peters church on the right. The Tramway Department's responsibility for paving 18"(457mm) each side of the track is clearly depicted. (Ipswich Transport Museum)

60.   Looking in the opposite direction the rail crossing can be seen again with sailing barges on the tidal River Orwell to the left and Vernon Street in the far distance over Stoke Bridge. The local coal order office completes the picture. (Ipswich Transport Museum)

61.   An unidentified car has left Bridge Street and crosses the graceful Stoke Bridge over the River Orwell and is about to enter Vernon Street on its way to Wherstead Road in the early 1920's. This cast iron bridge, built in 1818/19, was designed by William Cubitt, Chief Engineer of Ransomes and was replaced by the current concrete structure in 1924/25. The old maltings buildings on the right are now apartments and were used as barracks during the Napoleonic Wars. (Ipswich Transport Museum)

FROM WHERSTEAD RD.
(RAILWAY BRIDGE.)
To CORNHILL (via Queen Street)

WEEK DAYS.			SUNDAYS.	
a.m.	p.m.	p.m.	p.m.	p.m.
7 35	1 4	7 4	12 34	7 4
7 49	1 19	7 19	12 49	7 19
8 4	1 34	7 34	1 4	7 34
8 19	1 49	7 49	1 19	7 49
8 34	2 4	8 4	1 34	8 4
8 49	2 10	8 19	1 49	8 19
9 4	2 34	8 34	2 4	8 34
9 19	2 49	8 49	2 19	8 49
9 34	3 4	9 4	2 34	9 4
9 49	3 19	9 19	2 49	9 19
10 4	3 34	9 34	3 4	9 34
10 19	3 49	9 49	3 19	9 49
10 34	4 4	10 4	3 34	10 4
10 49	4 19	10 19	3 49	10 15
11 4	4 34	10 34	4 4	
11 19	4 49	10 44	4 19	
11 34	5 4		4 34	
11 49	5 19		4 49	
p.m.	5 34		5 4	
12 4	5 49		5 19	
12 19	6 4		5 34	
12 34	6 19		5 49	
12 49	6 34		6 4	
	6 49		6 19	
			6 34	
			6 49	

62.   The "Old Bell" Corner, with the named public house in this view. Vernon Street is on the left and Stoke Street is on the right, which is an extension of Burrell Road leading from the Station. To the rear of the photographer is Stoke Bridge. Whilst the replacement concrete bridge was being built in 1924/25, tram access to Vernon Street could have only been via the Station and Burrell Road/Stoke Street. However the only tram route to the Station from the town centre had been converted to trolleybus in 1923 and most of the track lifted the following year. Two trams were therefore left on the isolated section of track to provide a shuttle service between the Station and Wherstead Road until the new bridge was opened with the introduction of trolleybuses to replace the trams on this route. (Author's postcard)

63.   This view of Vernon Street is unrecognisable today with buildings on both sides of the road demolished and replaced by miscellaneous properties on the left and flats on the right. Car 26 is seen on single track with the end of double track in the foreground. The photographer appears to have taken the picture from the upper deck of an adjacent tram. (Author's postcard)

Bath Street/Wherstead Road

64.   This poor view is the only one located which shows the branch off Wherstead Road along Bath Street, which led to the quayside of the River Orwell. The branch transported passengers from the town centre to join the paddle steamers that travelled down the river to Felixstowe/Harwich and also served the employees of the Ransomes and Rapier factory at their Waterside Works. Due to the shortage of steel during the 1914-18 War the track was lifted in 1917 to provide much needed replacements elsewhere on the system and was never reinstated. (Author's postcard)

➔ 65. This view depicts the three Great Eastern Railway paddle steamers, namely *Norfolk*, *Suffolk* and *Essex*, with two on the left hand Bath Street side of the River Orwell and the third on the right next to the Promenade walkway, which ran between the river and the dock basin. The steamers could not turn in the river so they were double bow ended very much like the trams. No pictures have been discovered that include an Ipswich tram at the end of Bath Street with a steamer in the background or visa versa. The paddle steamer service ran from 1895 to 1930. (Author's postcard)

➔   66. Here is a replica of the publicity produced by the Great Eastern Railway for its rail and steamer excursions from Ipswich to Felixstowe and Harwich. It should perhaps read "Combined Rail, Tram and Steamer Excursions". (Author's collection)

GREAT EASTERN RAILWAY

COMBINED RAIL & STEAMER EXCURSIONS

WESTERFIELD
IPSWICH
DERBY ROAD
ORWELL
RIVER ORWELL
PIN MILL
TRIMLEY
FELIXSTOWE TOWN
BEACH
RIVER STOUR
PARKESTON QUAY
PIER
WRABNESS
HARWICH
DOVERCOURT BAY
North Sea

ESSEX

WELL-APPOINTED PADDLE STEAMERS "NORFOLK" "SUFFOLK" & "ESSEX"

FELIXSTOWE TO IPSWICH AND BACK FROM 1/1d.

ROUND TRIP BY BOAT AND TRAIN FROM ONLY 1/6d.

STEAMERS ALSO CALL AT HARWICH & PIN MILL

67.	At the Wherstead Road terminus on the town side of Bourne Bridge Cars 21 and 2, devoid of advertisements, wait to return to the town centre in the summer of 1904. The Edwardian couple present a smart image in their period clothes. (Ipswich Transport Museum)

TO IPSWICH STATION

Princes Street

68.   Amongst the atmosphere of this animated scene Car 32 moves down the top of Princes Street having just left Cornhill on its way to the Station circa 1904/05. The building to the right on the corner of Queen Street now houses Barclays Bank. (Author's postcard)

69.   Car 15 has come to grief and has been derailed at the top of Princes Street opposite Queen Street. The incident has attracted a large crowd with a policeman in attendance as the fitter strives to deal with the derailed truck. The car to the rear with the indicator showing "To Car Shed" has been called upon to help. (Ipswich Transport Museum)

→   70. Car 7 moves down Princes Street passing the head of Queen Street on the right and the Corn Exchange building on the left. (Author's postcard)

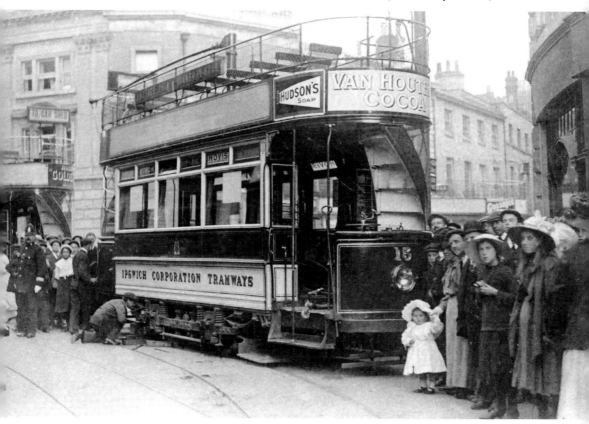

→   71. Car 1 poses on the double bend in Princes Street, together with interested bystanders. The building on the right was owned by wholesale druggist Grimwade Ridley and is now the site of the modern dark glazed offices of Willis Faber. The Fraser building, to the rear of the tram, and adjacent property were destroyed by fire in April 1912 and revealed the inadequacies of the borough's horse drawn fire brigade. (Author's postcard)

← 72. This view of Princes Street has been included to show the Fraser building before the fire with Car 25 making its way towards Cornhill. (Author's postcard)

73. This view shows the effects of the April 1912 fire on one of the traction standards that carried the overhead wiring. The destroyed building was the Waterloo Hotel, which was adjacent to the Fraser building. The effects of the fire and/or falling masonry have bent the traction standard double and the workmen in the foreground appear to be dismantling the bracket arm that carried the overhead. (Author's postcard)

74. This view depicts a scene that could be seen in many towns well into the 1950s when livestock was driven to town centre cattle markets. Here Car 1 appears to be driving the pigs towards the Princes Street cattle market. The advertisement indicates the longevity of Robertson's Golden Shred marmalade. (Ipswich Transport Museum)

Ipswich Station

75.   Although this circa 1904/05 view of the station approach has appeared in a number of publications it was felt worthy of repeating here. Car 10 appears to be leaving for the Cornhill on the left hand track with the boom on the correct right hand overhead wire. Car 14 has arrived and taken the right hand track; one of the crew looks skywards at a possible de-wirement or in anticipation on swinging the boom round ready for the return journey. (Author's postcard)

TRAMS AND SILENCE

IPSWICH'S NARROW STREETS AND NOISE

"If the authorities are really anxious to reduce traffic noises, and it would appear to be so since they are consistently worrying motorcyclists concerning their silencers, they might turn their attention to electric trams, which are deafening in certain districts." A correspondent in sending us the above, cut from a cycling paper, writes that he was recently staying in Ipswich, which struck him as being the worst town for street noises that he had ever visited, and that the trams were responsible for most of it.

We quite agree with our correspondent, but fear that the narrowness of the streets helps to concentrate the noises. If he were an enemy we would invite him to spend a day shut up in a room facing Carr Street. The noise made by the rushing past of trams, over broken rails, is an abomination.

21st April 1921   Editor

76.   Car 26, possibly on test, has just turned off the bridge over the River Orwell in Princes Street and into Burrell Road adjacent to the railway station forecourt; the Station Hotel is on the right. After recent rainfall the roadway looks in a fairly muddy condition.
(Author's postcard)

THE ALARM AT IPSWICH

In connection with yesterday's air raid Ipswich received warning by siren, in accordance with the advertised plan, that an enemy raid was taking place somewhere on the East Coast. Through the over zealous action of an official of the local tramways service the cars throughout the borough were stopped and sent to the station, but when this came to the knowledge of the Engineer and Manager (Mr Ayton) he promptly ordered them out again and the service was resumed.

6th June 1917

77.   Almost at the same location we see a further example of a horse bus of the Ipswich Omnibus Service which provided competition for the horse tramway; this ceased with the introduction of the electric trams. The horses are facing towards the bridge over the river and Ranelagh Road lies beyond the horsebus. Note that the company advertises the hire of brakes, waggonettes and cobs/ponies. (Author's postcard)

78.   An unidentified car waits outside the station forecourt, together with two boater-hatted cyclists, ready for the return to Cornhill. The station is in Burrell Road and the track in the foreground curves onto the river bridge over the River Orwell in Princes Street. In the background stands an open carriage and a railway delivery van whilst the central roof structure of the station appears to house a bell. (Author's postcard)

79.   A view in the opposite direction shows Car 25 on layover with a typical bracket arm, complete with double gas lamp, in the foreground. The full extent of the station canopy can be seen, whilst the conductor on the top deck appears to be swinging the boom round ready for the return journey to the town centre. (Author's postcard)

80.   The horse drawn vehicles wait outside the Station Hotel, which is opposite the railway station. Passengers board the horse tram, possibly rebuilt from a single deck car, which will turn right over the river bridge and along Princes Street. The patient horse on the right awaits its owner who is perhaps enjoying the hospitality of the hotel. (Ipswich Transport Museum)

TO WHITTON/BRAMFORD ROAD

Westgate Street/St Matthews Street/Barrack Corner

81.   Car 28 has just left Cornhill and entered Westgate Street with the premises of County Studios on the right next to the shop displaying bathtubs. On the opposite side of the road note the gas lamp cantilevered above the shop front. (Ipswich Transport Museum)

82. A busy scene in Westgate Street with two unidentified cars in view. Note the gas lamps on the outside of the shop on the right, which were used to illuminate the shop window during the hours of darkness. A little further along there are two strategically placed lamps on the edge of the pavement presumably opposite the public hall that was burnt down in 1948.
(Author's postcard)

→ 83. A little further along Westgate Street Car 29 is about to overtake the hand barrow and then travel along St Matthews Street and Norwich Road before turning into Bramford Road.
(Ipswich Transport Museum)

→ 84. Car 19 makes its way along St Matthews Street towards Westgate Street with the indicator showing the Wherstead Road/Felixstowe Road service, suggesting it had travelled via the station and then Portman Road, Mill Street and Barrack Corner, or is outward from the depot. To the right is a Home and Colonial grocery store plus a notice mounted on the traction standard exhorting people to "Use electric light. Present low rate 4d per unit less 5%". The scene is much changed today, with the top of Civic Drive where the gable ended building on the left stands.
(Author's postcard)

85.   Here we are at Barrack Corner with Car 17 moving into St Matthews Street. A triangular junction was formed here with track to the rear of the photographer leading into Norwich Road and the other two sides of the triangle joining to give access to Mill Street (later Portman Road) on the right. The large house on the right still stands today and was once owned by Richard Dykes Alexander, Banker and Philanthropist, and subsequently by his nephew William Dillwyn Sims, a partner in the local firm of Ransomes, Sims and Jeffries. The Half Moon and Star Hotel building still exists but is now a private residence. (D Kindred collection)

86.   This rather poor view has been included to show a single deck horse tram at Barrack Corner. The large house in the background is that illustrated in the previous picture. The track to the right leads into Mill Street that later became part of Portman Road. (Ipswich Transport Museum)

Norwich Road/Whitton

87. Car 4 departs from Barrack Corner and enters Norwich Road on its way to Whitton from Derby Road Station. A sign of the changing times is the advertising board on the building on the right indicating the sale of petrol. The track on the left leads towards Mill Street. (Ipswich Transport Museum)

88. Car 14 or 24 moves along Norwich Road towards St Matthews Street and the town centre and then onwards to Lattice Barn having left the passing loop adjacent to Granville Street. The local grocer A F Sawer, whose premises are on the left just beyond the tram, has taken advantage of the occasion to advertise his business by strategically positioning his delivery boy and bicycle. (Author's postcard)

➜ 89. Further along Norwich Road, near to Wellington Street, Car 36 is seen outward bound traversing a passing loop. The track points were spring loaded in favour of an approaching tram and were moved over by the wheels of vehicles travelling in the opposite direction. (Author's postcard)

➜ 90. Car 10 moves along an otherwise deserted Norwich Road at the junction of Wellington Street as it makes its way to Cornhill and thence to Derby Road Station. (Author's postcard)

91. Car 20 poses for an official photograph whilst completing a trial trip in November 1903 on Norwich Road next to the junction with Kitchener Road. This view again illustrates the motorman's restricted view to his left caused by the reverse staircase. Also note the dirty condition of the road.
(Author's postcard)

➔ 92. Car 33 poses for an official photograph in what is thought to be Norwich Road circa 1904/05. It is suggested the gentleman standing next to the car maybe the then General Manager, Mr Frank Ayton.
(Ipswich Transport Museum)

➔ 93. In this view one of the two under bridges that the Ipswich system had to cope with is shown. This is Norwich Road railway bridge, which carried the line to Felixstowe and the East Suffolk Line, looking towards Whitton. The other under bridge was on Wherstead Road. Car 20 poses under the bridge as Great Eastern Railway locomotive 1884 moves towards Ipswich Station having passed Westerfield Junction where the two branch lines split. Note the overhead has been offset given the limited passenger headroom under the bridge thus keeping them away from live wiring. (Author's postcard)

94.   Car 36, carrying the highest fleet number of the system, waits next to Norwich Road railway bridge before returning to Derby Road Station. The track stretches along the undeveloped road towards Whitton, whilst the notice on the bridge side indicates "Passengers are requested to keep to their seats whilst the car passes under the bridge". So much for Health and Safety! (R Marshall collection)

➜ 95. The Whitton terminus depicts Cars 14 and 24 on parallel track with 24 ready to depart to Cornhill and thence to Derby Road Station. The Maypole pub is on the extreme left beyond Car 14. (Author's postcard)

➜ 96. This posed view depicts Car 31 at the Whitton terminus with the Maypole public house on the left. In the background the local policeman has put in an appearance and the conductor stands at the beginning of the passing loop. Note the cast iron base of the traction standard in the foreground. (Author's postcard)

TRAMWAY TIME TABLE.
FROM WHITTON
To NORWICH ROAD (Railway Bridge), CORNHILL and LATTICE BARN.

	WEEK DAYS.			SATURDAYS ONLY.		SUNDAYS	
	a.m.	p.m.	p.m.	p.m.	p.m.	p.m.	p.m.
Route 9—BLUE Light.	7 56	12 28	6 28	5 40	8 52	12 44	6 40
	8 16	1 4	7 4	6 4	9 16	1 14	7 16
	8 42	1 40	7 40	6 28	9 40	1 52	7 52
	8 58	2 16	8 16	6 52	10 4	2 28	8 28
	9 28	3 52	8 52	7 16	10 40*	3 4	9 4
	10 4	3 28	9 28	7 40		3 40	9 40
	10 40	4 4	10 4	8 4		4 16	10 16†
	11 16	4 40	10 40*	8 28		4 52	
	11 52	5 16				5 28	
		5 52				6 4	

*To Cornhill only.   † To Barrack Corner only.

97.   This view depicts a poor children's outing organised by the RAOB (The Royal Antidiluvian Order of Buffaloes) on 25th August 1909. Twelve trams (six in view, headed by Car 12) were used to take 1,000 children from Princes Street to Whitton Crown Meadow where this photograph was taken. This children's outing looks as if it is in for a disappointing wet day given the raised umbrella and puddles. The trams in this view now carry advertisements with the one in the foreground appropriately featuring umbrellas. (Author's collection)

Bramford Road

98.   This view looks down the incline of Bramford Road from the direction of Norwich Road and with Wilberforce Street on the left. Ornate bracket arms carry the overhead wiring and the paved area each side of the track, which was the costly responsibility of the Tramway Department, is again well illustrated. The corner shop of J.Steel has a good display of kitchen hardware and crockery; the property is now a private residence. (Author's postcard)

99. Car 13, with a black on white route indicator, leaves the passing loop at the end of Prospect Road before beginning the climb up Bramford Road to its junction with Norwich Road. Beyond the sign for the Spotted Cow public house is a further example of the bracket arm carrying the overhead. (Ipswich Transport Museum; commercial postcard)

100. Car 13 is seen again about to enter the passing loop, seen in the previous picture, on its way to Cornhill and onwards to Lattice Barn. The building in the left background with a spire is the old Bramford Road School, which now houses the Suffolk Record Office. Although the scene has changed over the years, the terraced houses beyond the three storey premises on the right still exist. (Author's postcard)

101.   Further along Bramford Road Car 31 makes its way towards town with the Red Lion Inn on the right. In the background is the original railway bridge that carried the East Suffolk and Felixstowe lines from central Ipswich; because of its low height the trams terminated on the town side of the bridge. Also note the donkey cart in the foreground.
(Author's postcard)

102.   The crew of Car 12 pose for the photographer in the early 1920's confirmed by the destination displayed in the middle saloon window. The location is thought to be Bramford Road.
(Ipswich Transport Museum)

103.   The gleaming paintwork of Car 2, and the smartly dressed motorman, are a credit to the department in this view of the Bramford Road terminus taken circa 1904/05. The bridge in the background carried the line to Felixstowe and the East Suffolk Line but was too low for trams. When the trams were replaced in 1926 the route was extended under the bridge to Adair Road using single deck trolleybuses. (D Mackley collection)

FROM BRAMFORD RD.
To CORNHILL & DERBY RD. STATION

WEEK DAYS.			SUNDAYS.	
a.m.	p.m.	p.m.	p.m.	p.m.
7 8	12 2	6 2	12 28	6 50
7 21	12 14	6 12	12 43	7 2
7 35	12 26	6 26	12 58	7 14
7 42	12 38	6 38	1 13	7 26
7 52	12 50	6 50	1 26	7 38
8 3	1 2	7 2	1 38	7 50
8 14	1 14	7 14	1 50	8 2
8 26	1 26	7 26	2 2	8 14
8 38	1 38	7 38	2 14	8 26
8 50	1 50	7 50	2 26	8 38
9 2	2 2	8 2	2 38	8 50
9 14	2 14	8 14	2 50	9 2
9 26	2 26	8 26	3 2	9 14
9 38	2 38	8 38	3 14	9 26
9 50	2 50	8 50	3 26	9 38
10 2	3 2	9 2	3 38	9 50
10 14	3 14	9 14	3 50	10 0†
10 26	3 26	9 26	4 2	10 10*
10 38	3 38	9 38	4 14	10 15*
10 50	3 50	9 50	4 26	
11 2	4 2	10 2	4 38	
11 14	4 14	10 14	4 50	
11 26	4 26	10 20	5 2	
11 38	4 38	10 30	5 14	
11 50	4 50	10 42	5 26	
	5 2		5 38	
	5 14		5 50	
	5 26		6 2	
	5 38		6 14	
	5 50		6 26	
			6 38	

* To Barrack Corner only
† Cornhill only.   Route 2—WHITE Light.

DEPOTS

104.   The second Quadling Street horse tram depot is seen here when used by a haulage contractor.
The tram track was still in place when the site was redeveloped in the 1990's.
(Ipswich Transport Museum)

105.   An aerial view of the Constantine Road electric tram depot site with the running sheds and workshop to the top right of the large chimney stack. Immediately next to them, to the centre right, is the power station and to the left of the stack, the refuse destructor. At the bottom of the picture is the River Orwell, which was the source of cooling water for the power station together with the railway sidings bringing fuel for the boilers. (Ipswich Transport Museum)

106.   This view of the depot façade has four cars positioned in the doorway for the photographer. The depot, power station and refuse destructor were built on marshy ground and the chimney stack in the background required a substantial base to support the weight. (Ipswich Transport Museum)

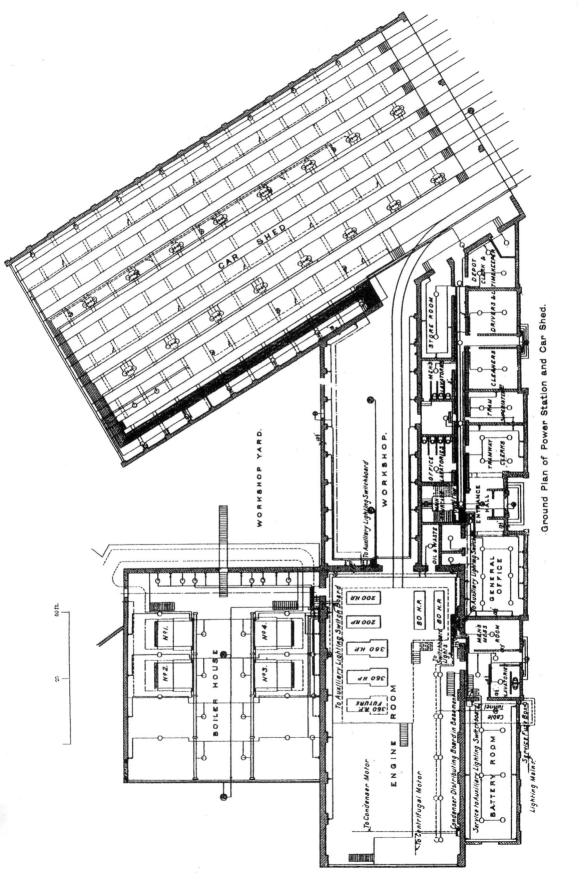

Ground Plan of Power Station and Car Shed.

CAR SHED.

WORKSHOP YARD.

WORKSHOP.

BOILER HOUSE.

Nº1. Nº2. Nº3. Nº4.

ENGINE ROOM.

BATTERY ROOM.

GENERAL OFFICE.

ENTRANCE HALL

STORE ROOM.

DEPOT CLERK & TIMEKEEPER.

DRIVERS &

CLEANERS.

TRAM SUPERINTENDENT.

TRAMWAY CLERKS

MEN'S LAVATORIES.

OFFICE

OIL & WASTE

MEN'S MESS ROOM

LAVATORIES

MEN'S MESS ROOM

360 H.P. FUTURE

360 H.P.

360 H.P.

200 H.P.

200 H.P.

80 H.P.

80 H.P.

To Condenser Motor.

To Centrifugal Motor.

Condenser Distributing Board in Basement.

Service to Auxiliary Lighting Switchboard.

Lighting Mains.

Service Fuse Board.

Cable Tunnel.

To Switchboard Lights.

To Auxiliary Lighting Switchboard

To Auxiliary Lighting Switchboard

To Auxiliary Lighting Switch

107.   Here we see inside Constantine Road depot before the opening of the electric system with ten Brush built car bodies supported on barrels awaiting the delivery and installation of the trucks. The supporting piers for the track in the pit area can be seen and the bodies of Cars 1 and 17 are identifiable. Also note the manufacture's advertising in the centre window.
(Author's postcard)

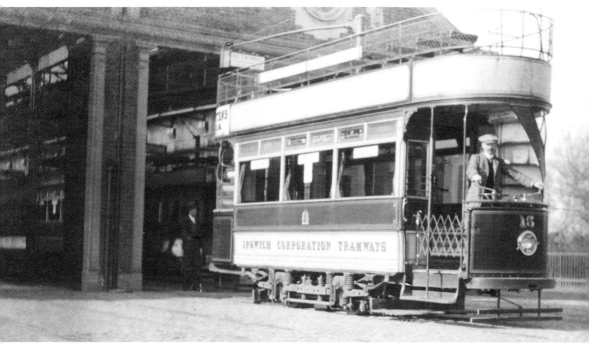

108.   Car 15 is seen outside the entrance to the depot with a motorman in civilian clothing complete with cloth cap. He may be a fitter or a member of the management who has brought the car out for the photographer. The view also provides a clear picture of the scissor guard used to close off the driving area.
(Author's collection)

IPSWICH TOWN COUNCIL

THE TRAMWAYMEN'S AGITATION

TRAMWAY EMPLOYEES' GRIEVANCES

The Electric Supply and Tramways Committee reported the receipt, on December 14th, of a statement giving the following "suggestions" for the tramway employees:

1. Five days work per week, at least, is required for every man employed during the winter months, on condition that none of the present staff are discharged on account of short time.

2. Suspensions for trivial offences to be abolished.

3. No man to stand on a car for more than five hours without relief during the winter months.

4. The relief sheets to be altered, so as to allow, everyman to have a mid-day meal, say between the hours of 12 and 3, or as near as possible.

5. During the winter months, neither regular nor relief turns to occupy more than ten hours, including reporting time.

6. Five minutes grace to be allowed on all reporting times.

7. A fresh agreement to be arranged between the Manaagement and the men, as to the time to be worked during the summer months and winter following on or before March 31st next.

8. The reinstatement of Motorman A J Smith.

STAFF

109.   A group photograph depicting some of the operating staff and their charges; on the left is Car 3 and to the right Car 14. The two centre cars have white on black route indicators whilst those on the outside are black on white; the date of the change is not known The view provides a good illustration of the overhead wiring into the depot. In the early 1900's working for the Corporation Tramway Department had a certain amount of status in the wider community even though the hours were long, wages poor and winter working conditions for the motormen atrocious.
(Ipswich Transport Museum)

← From this public notice it is apparent Motorman Smith was involved in an incident at the tramway depot in the early years of the system. He had been endeavouring to improve the working conditions of the staff and appears to have been dismissed for his activities; see Item 8 in the adjacent press cutting dating from February 1905. Also note the comments at the bottom of the poster and the harsh penalty for being 2 minutes late. (Ipswich Transport Museum)

110.   This group photograph of some of the motormen and conductors illustrates their smart turnout complete with white summer covers for their caps. The only exception is the lad on the right who was probably employed to change track and overhead points. (Ipswich Transport Museum)

111.   The men behind the scenes. This group of workers, positioned next to an electric tram, includes the Car Shed Foreman E Wolsey (third from the right on the back row) and skilled tradesmen covering trades, such as blacksmith and armature winder. The patriotic army recruitment poster in the side window, and the fact that the tram has been rebuilt, allows this view to be dated sometime towards the end of the 1914-18 War period. (Ipswich Transport Museum)

ROLLING STOCK

1903 1-26   1904 27-36   Brush "AA" 4 wheel truck   2 x Westinghouse 25 HP motors

112.   These 36 electric trams formed this small Ipswich fleet and were open topped with reverse staircases. There were 24 lower deck seats and 26 on the upper deck. The livery was dark green and cream with lining out as indicated in the photograph.

Initially destination boards were mounted on the decency boards (1904-06) and then moved to the upper deck guarding when advertisements were introduced. In addition, upper destination boxes were fitted at each end. These were removed and replaced by route number boxes fitted in 1922 with destinations displayed on the front dash and inside the middle saloon window.

As indicated earlier, six unidentified cars were sold to the Scarborough Tramway Company before the Ipswich system closed becoming their 23–28 and were scrapped in 1931. The company also purchased a tram body to replace one damaged in a serious accident. The Felixstowe Pier Company purchased Car 34. Car 33 is in an advanced state of restoration at the Ipswich Transport Museum and the remaining cars were either scrapped or used locally as sheds, summerhouses or workshops.

Municipal pride is illustrated in this view of an unidentified car outside Constantine Road depot. Both sides of the reverse staircases can be seen and the notice on the inward facing side of the destination box states "No Smoking Allowed Forward of the Trolley Standard"

In addition to the above, there was a works car/sweeper based on a Brush "A" 4 wheel truck but no photograph of this vehicle has come to light. (Ipswich Transport Museum)

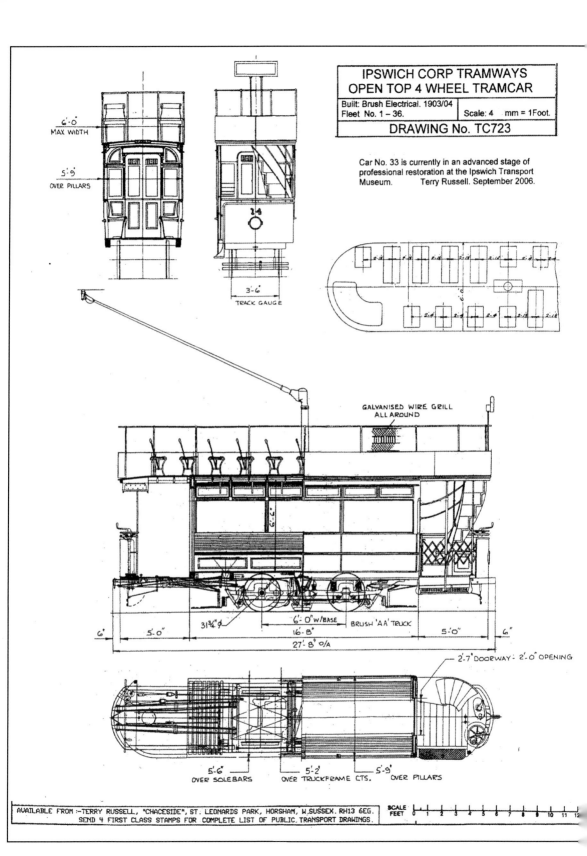

IPSWICH CORP TRAMWAYS
OPEN TOP 4 WHEEL TRAMCAR

Built: Brush Electrical. 1903/04
Fleet No. 1 – 36.

Scale: 4 mm = 1Foot.

DRAWING No. TC723

Car No. 33 is currently in an advanced stage of
professional restoration at the Ipswich Transport
Museum.   Terry Russell. September 2006.

6'-0"
MAX WIDTH

5'-9"
OVER PILLARS

3'-6"
TRACK GAUGE

14

GALVANISED WIRE GRILL
ALL AROUND

6"   5'-0"

31¾" Ø

6'-0" W/BASE
16'-8"
27'-8" O/A

BRUSH 'AA' TRUCK

5'-0"   6"

2'-7" DOORWAY: 2'-0" OPENING

5'-6"
OVER SOLEBARS

5'-2"
OVER TRUCKFRAME CTS.

5'-9"
OVER PILLARS

AVAILABLE FROM :–TERRY RUSSELL, "CHACESIDE", ST. LEONARDS PARK, HORSHAM, W.SUSSEX. RH13 6EG.
SEND 4 FIRST CLASS STAMPS FOR COMPLETE LIST OF PUBLIC TRANSPORT DRAWINGS.

SCALE
FEET   0 1 2 3 4 5 6 7 8 9 10 11 12

TOWER WAGON

113.   The Department's horse drawn tower wagon is seen here installing a traction standard or electricity distribution pole. The tramway and electricity departments were run as a single unit. The notes on the rear of this photograph indicate that the man on top of the tower is Joseph Kemp who was later killed when the horse providing motive power shied causing the wagon to topple over. The unit can be seen on display at the Ipswich Transport Museum, Cobham Road. (Ipswich Transport Museum)

TRAMS TO TROLLEYBUSES

114.   This view in Norwich Road shows trams being dismantled on the 27th July 1926. The body of Car 32 is supported on trestles whilst the truck is removed by horse power. The body will possibly be sold locally as a shed/workshop. By the time this photograph was taken the cars sold to the Scarborough Tramways Company had departed. Note the warning lamps in the road on the right and the differing route number blind colours between the two cars in the foreground. (Ipswich Transport Museum; commercial postcard)

TRACKLESS TRAMS FOR IPSWICH

The announcement that, with a view to economy, the trackless tram system is to be tried as an experiment at Ipswich, between the Cornhill and the Railway Station, marks an interesting departure, the result of which will be watched with interest. Months ago, when the tram controversy was at its height, the suggestion was made that this system should be given a trial, but the Tramway Committee took no action in that decision. Now, faced with the prospect of a heavy bill for track relaying and road repairs, the Committee has come to the conclusion that trackless trolley trams merit consideration, and three single deck cars, each to seat 30 persons, are to be hired as a experiment. The cars will be operated on the pay-as-you-enter principle, and the driver will also be the conductor, so the anticipated economy will not be confined to the track, but should be reflected also in the wage bill. It is not claimed that the Committee has at a blow evolved a means of turning the heavy annual tramway deficit into a profit, though if track expenditure can be cut the new plan should go a long way in this direction. As a means towards this very desirable end, there is ample justification for the experiment, the more so as the expenditure involved will not be more than £700, while certain of the material used in the adaptation can be utilised in replacements should the new scheme not achieve all that is desired of it.   10th August 1922

This cartoon was created in the Autumn of 1923 and provides a commentary on the poor state of the Ipswich track at that time plus a reference to the experimental "trackless trams" (i.e. trolleybuses). (Ipswich Transport Museum)

115. Once the trials with the three Railless trolleybuses between Cornhill and the Station had proved to be a success, the Corporation wasted no time in lifting the tram track along the majority of Princes Street. Here we see this work in progress at the junction with Portman Road on the left. Railless 1 passes the works on its way to Cornhill demonstrating its manoeuvrability with booms fully extended. Note the latter are connected to an early form of retriever and also the rear open area for smokers. The Churchman cigarette premises form the backdrop. (Ipswich Transport Museum)

116. Railless trolleybus 2 (now on display at the Ipswich Transport Museum) rounds the corner in the upper part of Princes Street. The right hand track has been removed (see Picture 71) as workmen prepare the new road surface; a section of the left hand track in the foreground has also been removed. The inclined pole appears to be supporting the traction standard on the right, which is perhaps being stressed by the extra set of overhead wiring being pulled off to create the curve for the booms. (Ipswich Transport Museum)

THE AFTER LIFE

117.   After the closure of the Ipswich system, Car 34 was sold to the nearby Felixstowe Pier Company who used it, minus top deck, plus the addition of a diesel engine and trailer. Here an earlier unit can be seen transporting members of the public to the end of the pier possibly to catch one of the Great Eastern Railway paddle steamers back to Ipswich. Today only a stub of the pier remains. (Ipswich Transport Museum)

← 118. As indicated in the opening system history, six cars were sold to the Scarborough Tramway Company in 1925 before the closure of the Ipswich system in 1926. (See *Scarborough Tramways.*) The next few views illustrate the ex Ipswich cars operating in their new Yorkshire home. The fleet numbers of the Ipswich cars sold to Scarborough are not known. Seen in the depot yard in July 1929 is an unidentified Ipswich car. A destination display has been added to the side of the dash panel and there are also many advertisements for the usual seaside attractions.
(E Cordukes; Burrows collection, Newham Museum)

← 119. Scarborough Cars 21 and 25 are seen in the depot yard in July 1929. The reverse staircase readily identifies these ex Ipswich cars. Note the destination box has been lowered and an additional display board mounted above. 21 used an Ipswich car body, in addition to the six complete vehicles purchased, in the rebuild of the Scarborough tram that was involved in a major accident in 1925. (E Cordukes; Burrows collection, Newham Museum)

120. This fine view by the Grand Pavilion in Scarborough depicts Car 24 waiting to make further progress, which appears to be prevented by the line of single deck motorbuses, notwithstanding the ex Ipswich car was 6" (152mm) narrower than the resident fleet. The between decks advertisement indicates "This Car Conveys You to & from the Passenger Steamers that Sail from the Lighthouse Pier", bringing back memories of the Ipswich route to the river paddle steamers. The film showing at the corner cinema is "The Cradle Snatchers". (Author's collection)

MP Middleton Press

EVOLVING THE ULTIMATE RAIL ENCYCLOPEDIA

Easebourne Lane, Midhurst, West Sussex.
GU29 9AZ   Tel:01730 813169

www.middletonpress.co.uk   email:info@middletonpress.co.uk
A-978 0 906520 B-978 1 873793 C-978 1 901706 D-978 1 904474 E-978 1 906008

OOP Out of print at time of printing - Please check availability   BROCHURE AVAILABLE SHOWING NEW TITLES